Everyday Robots

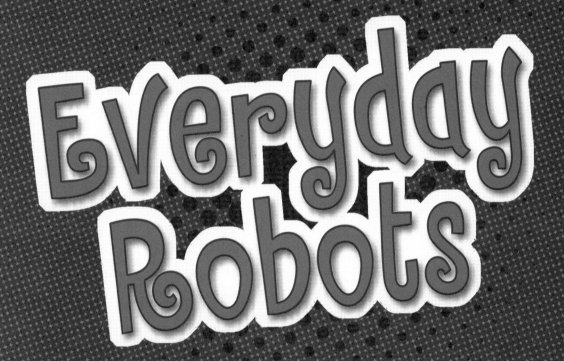

Katherine Lewis

Lerner Publications • Minneapolis

Copyright © 2021 by Lerner Publishing Group, Inc.

All rights reserved. International copyright secured. No part of this book may be reproduced, stored in a retrieval system, or transmitted in any form or by any means—electronic, mechanical, photocopying, recording, or otherwise—without the prior written permission of Lerner Publishing Group, Inc., except for the inclusion of brief quotations in an acknowledged review.

Lerner Publications Company
An imprint of Lerner Publishing Group, Inc.
241 First Avenue North
Minneapolis, MN 55401 USA

For reading levels and more information, look up this title at www.lernerbooks.com.

Main body text set in Billy Infant regular.
Typeface provided by SparkType.

Editor: Alison Lorenz

Library of Congress Cataloging-in-Publication Data

Names: Lewis, Katherine, 1996- author.
Title: Everyday robots / Katherine Lewis.
Description: Minneapolis : Lerner Publications, 2021. | Series: Lightning bolt books . Robotics | Includes bibliographical references and index. | Audience: Ages 6-9 | Audience: Grades 2-3 | Summary: "Robots can help people clean, mow their lawns, learn new things, and more. Young readers meet the robots making every day easier and discover which tasks helper robots will tackle next"— Provided by publisher.
Identifiers: LCCN 2019047615 (print) | LCCN 2019047616 (ebook) | ISBN 9781541596931 (library binding) | ISBN 9781728413570 (paperback) | ISBN 9781728400426 (ebook)
Subjects: LCSH: Robots—Juvenile literature.
Classification: LCC TJ211.2 .L49 2020 (print) | LCC TJ211.2 (ebook) | DDC 629.8/92—dc23

LC record available at https://lccn.loc.gov/2019047615
LC ebook record available at https://lccn.loc.gov/2019047616

Manufactured in the United States of America
1-47799-48239-1/10/2020

Table of Contents

What Is a Robot?

A robot cleans up while its owner relaxes. How does the robot work?

Some robots can help in the kitchen.

Robots are machines that can move. They have sensors. Different robots help people do different jobs. But all robots have much in common.

Sony's robotic dog, aibo, senses voices and movements.

Robot sensors sense light, sound, and touch. Robots use energy to move. They get energy from gas, batteries, or the sun.

Robots use computers to think. Engineers type instructions into the computers. These instructions are programs.

Different programs tell robots to do different jobs.

Robots at Home

Many people have robots at home. The robots do chores people don't like to do.

One kind of robot cleans floors. Its sensors can find dirt. The robot spends more time cleaning dirty spots.

Robot vacuums move around on their own. You can just relax!

Another kind of robot can mow lawns. Its sensors find the edges of the lawn. They help the robot avoid things such as trees and pets.

Some mower robots can even work in the rain!

A robot makes cleaning a pool much easier.

A different robot can clean pools. It can dive to the bottom to clean. Engineers are creating butler robots and other household robots too.

Personal Robots

Personal robots help people with daily tasks. One personal robot is a self-driving car. Sensors on the roof watch where the car is going.

A robotic alarm clock can help you wake up. It jumps off your nightstand. It rolls around and makes noise until you get up to turn it off.

This alarm clock robot, Clocky, can hide itself to make sure you get out of bed.

Some robots help people eat well or remember to take their medicine. One type of robot sits on the kitchen counter. It can answer questions about making healthful choices.

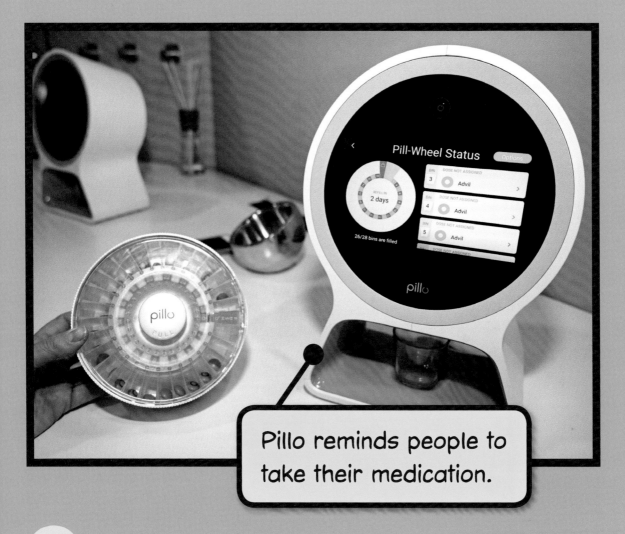

Pillo reminds people to take their medication.

People with diabetes often give themselves injections. One day, a robot might help.

Other robots can help people with disabilities move and reach. Robot wheelchairs have arms that can grab objects. Some robots can open doors, hold things, or even cook food.

Toy Robots

Toy robots can help kids learn how to solve problems. Kids can build, program, and run the robots.

LEGO makes kits to help kids learn about robots.

Robot kits help kids learn about robots. Kids use the robots to play games. The robots can crawl, kick, and throw. Some schools even have robot-building contests.

Kids can tell Sphero to spin and light up. They can even draw the robot a path to move along.

Kids program many kinds of robots. The robots can move, change colors, and more.

Toy robots help with more than just learning. They are also fun to use. Many kinds of robots help people every day!

Where do you see robots during the day?

Behind the Robot

A robot engineer is called a roboticist. People who become roboticists go to college for at least four years. They study science, math, computer programming, and design. Roboticists may spend the day reading diagrams, programming robots, or testing new sensors. They also talk with people who will use the robots. Roboticists who build household robots think about making the robots easy to use and fix.

Fun Facts

- Robot vacuums have sucked up more than 2 billion pounds (907 million kg) of dirt.

- For several years in Japan, travelers could check into a hotel staffed only by robots.

- Students at the University of Houston in Texas can have robots deliver food.

Glossary

butler: a household servant

engineer: a designer or builder of machines

program: a set of computer instructions

robot: a machine that does work for humans

robotic: related to robots

sensor: a part of a robot that lets it understand its environment

Further Reading

Gagne, Tammy. *Robots.* Minneapolis: POP, 2019.

Higgins, Nadia. *Robots at Home.* Mankato, MN: Amicus, 2018.

Robot Facts for Kids
https://kids.kiddle.co/Robot

Robotics
https://sciencetrek.org/sciencetrek/topics /robots/

Schaefer, Lola. *Robots on the Job.* Minneapolis: Lerner Publications, 2021.

Science Kids: Robots for Kids
http://www.sciencekids.co.nz/robots.html

Index

Photo Acknowledgments

Image credits: © clocky.com, pp. 2, 13; diego_cervo/istock/Getty Images, p. 4; wonry/Getty Images, p. 5; Larry French/Getty Images, p. 6; Maskot/Getty Images, p. 7; miriam-doerr/ Getty Images, pp. 8, 15; South_agency/Getty Images, p. 9; IKvyatkovskaya/Getty Images, p. 10; wakila/Getty Images, p. 11; ANGELO MERENDINO/AFP/Getty Images, p. 12; ROBYN BECK/AFP/Getty Images, p. 14; mediaphotos/Getty Images, p. 16; Mikhail Sedov/Getty Images, p. 17; Lewis Geyer/Digital First Media/Boulder Daily Camera/Getty Images, p. 18; Highwaystarz-Photography/Getty Images, p. 19; Westend61/Getty Images, p. 22.

Cover: Miriam Doerr Martin Frommherz/Shutterstock.com.